W9-AOY-983

BEASTLY BOOKS FOR THE BRAVE

THIS BOOK
HISSES!

CAITIE MCANENEY

Gareth Stevens
PUBLISHING

Please visit our website, www.garethstevens.com. For a free color catalog of all our high-quality books, call toll free 1-800-542-2595 or fax 1-877-542-2596.

Library of Congress Cataloging-in-Publication Data

Names: McAneney, Caitie, author.
Title: This book hisses! / Caitie McAneney.
Description: New York : Gareth Stevens Publishing, [2020] | Series: Beastly books for the brave | Includes bibliographical references and index.
Identifiers: LCCN 2018028882| ISBN 9781538233658 (library bound) | ISBN 9781538233634 (paperback) | ISBN 9781538233641 (6 pack)
Subjects: LCSH: Animal defenses--Juvenile literature.
Classification: LCC QL759 .M43 2020 | DDC 591.47--dc23
LC record available at https://lccn.loc.gov/2018028882

First Edition

Published in 2020 by
Gareth Stevens Publishing
111 East 14th Street, Suite 349
New York, NY 10003

Copyright © 2020 Gareth Stevens Publishing

Designer: Katelyn E. Reynolds
Editor: Kate Light

Photo credits: Cover, p. 1 (snake) iqbalzhu/Shutterstock.com; cover, pp. 1-24 (book cover) Ensuper/Shutterstock.com; cover, p. 1-24 (tape) Picsfive/Shutterstock.com; cover, pp. 1-24 (decorative elements) cute vector art/Shutterstock.com; cover, pp. 1-24 (book interior and wood background) robert_s/Shutterstock.com; pp. 4-21 (fun fact background) Miloje/Shutterstock.com; p. 5 (main) SNC Art and More/Shutterstock.com; p. 5 (inset) Phillip W. Kirkland/Shutterstock.com; p. 7 YuSafa/Shutterstock.com; p. 9 Yana Radysh/Shutterstock.com; p. 11 (main) apple2499/Shutterstock.com; p. 11 (inset) Suzi Eszterhas/Minden Pictures/Getty Images; p. 13 (Texas horned lizard) Danita Delmont/Shutterstock.com; p. 13 (frilled lizard) Matt Cornish/Shutterstock.com; p. 13 (green iguana) Patrick K. Campbell/Shutterstock.com; p. 13 (horned lizards) Wild Horizons/UIG via Getty Images; pp. 14, 18 Ridvan EFE/Shutterstock.com; p. 15 Milan Zygmunt/Shutterstock.com; p. 17 Jason Mintzer/Shutterstock.com; p. 19 Aleksey Stemmer/Shutterstock.com; p. 21 Photography by Adri/Shutterstock.com.

Printed in the United States of America

CPSIA compliance information: Batch #CS19GS: For further information contact Gareth Stevens, New York, New York at 1-800-542-2595.

CONTENTS

WORDS IN THE GLOSSARY APPEAR IN **BOLD** TYPE THE FIRST TIME THEY ARE USED IN THE TEXT.

IT'S A WARNING!

Imagine you go to pet a cat. Its ears go back. Its eyes narrow. It spreads its mouth wide and lets out a big *hiss*. What's that? It's a warning!

Many animals use hissing to warn the people and animals around them to *back off*. This **defense** is used by both big predators and smaller prey. **Reptiles** such as snakes, **mammals** such as tigers, and bugs such as cockroaches all make this **intimidating** sound. It might be your last chance to get away!

FACTS FOR THE FEARLESS

RACCOONS, OPOSSUMS, AND RATS HISS TO MAKE THEMSELVES SEEM SCARY TO PREDATORS.

HISSING OPOSSUM

RACCOONS MIGHT LOOK CUTE AND CUDDLY, BUT YOU SHOULD ALWAYS BE CAREFUL AROUND WILD ANIMALS!

TARANTULAS HISS!

Not many animals want to mess with a tarantula. They can defend themselves with a painful, **venomous** bite. However, before they attack, they often send a warning to their predators.

When a tarantula feels **threatened**, it will make a buzzing or hissing sound. It makes this noise by rubbing its hairy legs together! The tarantula may also lean back and lift up its front legs. This is the tarantula's way of saying it's ready to attack if an animal comes any closer.

FACTS FOR THE FEARLESS

AN ADAPTATION IS A CHANGE IN A TYPE OF ANIMAL THAT MAKES IT BETTER ABLE TO LIVE IN ITS SURROUNDINGS. TARANTULAS HAVE LOTS OF TERRIFYING ADAPTATIONS!

TARANTULA ADAPTATIONS AND DEFENSES

SPINERETS
PRODUCE SILK

ABDOMEN
LETS GO OF SPECIAL HAIRS
THAT CAN HURT THE EYES
AND NOSE OF ATTACKERS

EIGHT EYES
USED FOR HUNTING

LEG HAIRS
SENSE SMALL MOVEMENTS
IN THE GROUND; MAKE A
HISSING SOUND WHEN LEGS
RUB TOGETHER

FANGS
CAN DELIVER
A VENOMOUS BITE

WOULD YOU DARE TO KEEP A TARANTULA AS A PET?

7

HISSING HOUSE CATS

You've probably met this next hissing beast—a house cat! They might hiss before biting or scratching a person or animal who gets too close. They might hiss to let other cats know they're **dominant.** Sometimes they hiss out of fear. It's the cat's way of setting a **boundary.** They don't want to be touched, or else!

Some **experts** who study cats think they might hiss to sound like a snake. Many snakes are known to be deadly. This sound terrifies people and animals alike!

FACTS FOR THE FEARLESS

SMALL CATS ARE SOME OF THE DEADLIEST KILLERS IN AMERICA. IN 2013, IT WAS FOUND THEY KILL BILLIONS OF MAMMALS AND BIRDS EVERY YEAR.

PET CATS MIGHT LOOK FLUFFY AND CUTE. BUT DON'T BE MISTAKEN! THEY'RE GREAT HUNTERS AND WILL ATTACK IF THEY GET SCARED!

9

BIG CATS, BIG TROUBLE

Believe it or not, big cats hiss, too! And when they hiss, it can mean big trouble.

Tigers are the largest of all cat species, or kinds. Adults can be up to 6 feet (1.8 m) long and weigh more than 700 pounds (317.5 kg).

You don't want to mess with a tiger! They're master hunters of the night. They sneak up behind prey, then strike at the throat. Tigers hiss and snarl when they're being **aggressive** or defensive.

FACTS FOR THE FEARLESS

SNOW LEOPARDS CAN HISS WHEN THEY'RE ANGRY. BUT, UNLIKE OTHER BIG CATS, SNOW LEOPARDS DON'T ROAR.

CHEETAHS OFTEN HISS DURING A FIGHT. STAY AWAY FROM THIS SPEEDY FELINE!

TIGERS MAKE LOTS OF SOUNDS BESIDES HISSING! THEY ALSO ROAR, GROWL, AND MOAN. YOU CAN HEAR A TIGER'S ROAR FROM 2 MILES (3.2 KM) AWAY!

LIZARDS WITH ATTITUDE

Hissing cats aren't that strange, but what about hissing reptiles? Some lizards hiss to keep predators away. Like cats, lizards often open their mouth while hissing to show off their teeth.

The blue-tongued skink is a common Australian species. When faced with a possible predator, the skink will puff up its body to look larger. Then, it'll let out a warning hiss. It also sticks out its blue tongue! The strange color surprises the predator, and the skink gets away.

FACTS FOR THE FEARLESS

When scared, a lizard called the goanna will stand on its back legs, make its neck look bigger, and hiss loudly.

OTHER WEIRD LIZARD DEFENSES

TEXAS HORNED LIZARD

THE TEXAS HORNED LIZARD SHOOTS BLOOD OUT OF ITS EYES!

FRILLED LIZARD

THE FRILLED LIZARD PUFFS OUT ITS SKIN FLAP AND RUNS ON ITS BACK LEGS!

GREEN IGUANAS

GREEN IGUANAS USE THEIR LONG TAILS TO WHIP ATTACKERS!

HORNED LIZARDS

HORNED LIZARDS FILL THEMSELVES WITH AIR TO LOOK LIKE A SPIKY BALLOON!

REAL-LIFE MONSTERS

The Gila (HEE-luh) monster lurks underground. The black, scaly creature only comes out to sit in the sun or to hunt. When you see one, stay away! This lizard earned its scary name. It's venomous!

Luckily, the Gila monster warns before it strikes predators or other Gila monsters. It flicks its snakelike tongue. It snorts and hisses. That means get away! If you don't, the Gila monster may strike. As it bites down, its venom goes into its victim.

UNITED STATES

MEXICO

GILA MONSTER RANGE

GILA MONSTERS CAN HAVE YELLOW, ORANGE, OR PINK PARTS ON THEIR SCALES. THESE LIZARDS ARE FOUND IN THE DESERTS OF NORTHWESTERN MEXICO AND THE SOUTHWESTERN UNITED STATES.

SNAKE SOUNDS

Snakes are some of the scariest hissing creatures. The inland taipan, king cobra, and black mamba are some of the deadliest animals in the world! With their signature hiss, most people and animals know to keep their distance.

Some snakes hiss when they're scared. Hissing makes smaller snakes seem like bigger threats. Snakes hiss as a defense by letting out air quickly through a part in their throat called a glottis. Snakes can also growl and shriek!

FACTS FOR THE FEARLESS

ANOTHER DEFENSE OF A SCARED SNAKE IS... PASSING GAS! THEY LET OUT GAS TO MAKE A SOUND TO SCARE WOULD-BE PREDATORS.

When threatened, a rattlesnake will shake its noisy tail, let out a hiss, and raise its head up high. It's ready to attack!

CREEPY COCKROACHES

Have you ever heard a bug hiss? Probably not! That doesn't mean it's impossible. The Madagascar hissing cockroach is famous for its strange hissing sound. This cockroach hisses by **exhaling** through breathing holes in its body.

Madagascar hissing cockroaches hiss when sounding an alarm. They also hiss while fighting one another. Scientists think the winners of the fight hiss more than the losers. The males also hiss for another reason: to draw in a female!

AFRICA

MADAGASCAR

■ MADAGASCAR HISSING COCKROACH RANGE

MADAGASCAR HISSING COCKROACHES LIVE ON THE FOREST FLOOR IN MADAGASCAR, AN ISLAND OFF OF SOUTHEASTERN AFRICA. YOU CAN USUALLY FIND THEM AT A ZOO!

LISTEN UP!

Animals have different ways of letting people and other animals know when they're happy, scared, or ready to attack. From big cats to cockroaches, hissing is a universal language. Listen up!

Hissing is an important defense for creatures across the animal kingdom. Some animals use it when they feel scared or threatened. Some use it to make themselves seem bigger than they are. For many, it's a warning that they can kill. Even the brave know when to listen to wild warnings!

EVEN GEESE WILL HISS IN DEFENSE!

GLOSSARY

aggressive: acting with forceful energy and determination. Also, showing a readiness to attack.

boundary: something that marks the limit of an area or place

defense: a way of guarding against an enemy

dominant: the most powerful or strongest

exhale: to breathe out

expert: someone who knows a great deal about something

intimidating: creating a feeling of fear or awe in a person or animal

mammal: a warm-blooded animal that has a backbone and hair, breathes air, and feeds milk to its young

reptile: an animal covered with scales or plates that breathes air, has a backbone, and lays eggs

threaten: to do something that is likely to cause harm to someone or something. Also, a sign of danger.

venomous: able to produce a liquid called venom that is harmful to other animals

FOR MORE INFORMATION

BOOKS

Kroll, Jennifer L. *Showdown: Animal Defenses*. Huntington Beach, CA: Teacher Created Materials, 2018.

Morey, Allan. *Frilled Lizards*. Mankato, MN: Amicus High Interest, Amicus Ink, 2018.

National Geographic Kids. *Everything Big Cats*. Washington, DC: National Geographic, 2018.

WEBSITES

Fun Cat Facts for Kids
www.sciencekids.co.nz/sciencefacts/animals/cat.html
Discover fun facts about a hissing master—the house cat!

Gila Monster
kids.nationalgeographic.com/animals/gila-monster/#gila-monster-emerging-ground.jpg
Explore more about the hissing Gila monster!

Hissing Cockroach
kids.nationalgeographic.com/animals/hissing-cockroach/#HissingCockroach1.jpg
Read about the creepy crawly Madagascar hissing cockroach!

INDEX